T

D0200792

From:

KEEP CALM

AND

HAVE A CUPCAKE

SWEET LITTLE THOUGHTS ON STAYING SANE

Written and compiled by
Evelyn Beilenson and Lois Kaufman

 PETER PAUPER PRESS, INC.
White Plains, New York

Illustrated and designed
by Margaret Rubiano

Graphic illustration on jacket, page 1, and page 3
copyright © Jenny Heid and Aaron Nieradka.

Copyright © 2010
Peter Pauper Press, Inc.
202 Mamaroneck Avenue
White Plains, NY 10601
All rights reserved
ISBN 978-1-4413-0327-1
Printed in China
14   13

Visit us at www.peterpauper.com

KEEP
CALM
AND
HAVE A
CUPCAKE
SWEET LITTLE THOUGHTS
ON STAYING SANE

introduction

Short and sweet—just like cupcakes — this little compendium is a cookbook for comfort. If there's a recipe for happiness, an essential ingredient would be simple pleasures in large measure. Like the aroma of home-baked goodies wafting through childhood memories, these servings of sanity in the midst of a busy world warm the heart.

Life's a batch.
Eat cupcakes.

Auburn Hutton

So long as
there is food in
the mouth, so long
will the words
be sweet.

Hindu proverb

The cure for anything is a cupcake and a cup of tea.

Lois Kaufman

If hunger makes
you irritable, better
eat and be pleasant.

Talmud

Food, like a loving touch or a glimpse of divine power, has that ability to comfort.

Norman Kolpas

It is the sweet,
simple things of
life which are the
real ones after all.

Laura Ingalls Wilder

Create your comforts
anew each morning, like
fresh-baked cupcakes.

Barbara Paulding

Food is our common ground, a universal experience.

James Beard

This is what baking . . .
is about: feeling good,
wafting along in the
warm, sweet-smelling air,
unwinding, no longer being
entirely an office creature;
and that's exactly what I
mean when I talk about
"comfort cooking."

Nigella Lawson

Let's toast our lives
with cupcakes and tea—
One for you and two
for me!

Author unknown

Food responds
to our soul's
dream as to
our stomach's
appetite.

Joseph Delteil

Soul is our appetite,
driving us to eat from the
banquet of life. People
filled with the hunger of
soul take food from every
dish before them, whether
it be sweet or bitter.

Matthew Fox

Whenever you
are sincerely
pleased, you
are nourished.

Ralph Waldo Emerson

An exquisite pleasure had invaded my senses. . . . Whence could it have come to me, this all-powerful joy? I sensed that it was connected with the taste of the tea and the cake. . . .

Remembrance of Things Past,

Marcel Proust

One cannot think
well, love well,
sleep well, if one
has not dined well.

Virginia Woolf

If you're going to eat a cupcake, make it chocolate. Chocoholics live longer than others, and besides, chocolate is an aphrodisiac!

Author unknown

A good cupcake and
a good life have many of
the same ingredients—
good timing, sugar,
and spice.

Evelyn Beilenson

Food is the most primitive form of comfort.

Sheila Graham

Come along inside—
we'll see if tea and
cupcakes can make the
world a better place.

*(with apologies to
Kenneth Grahame)*

If you must eat vegetables, have a carrot cupcake.

Lois Kaufman

My kitchen is a mystical place, a kind of temple for me. It is a place where the surfaces seem to have significance, where the sounds and odors carry meaning that transfers from the past and bridges to the future.

Pearl Bailey

Food to a large extent is what holds a society together and eating is closely linked to deep spiritual experiences.

Peter Farb and
George Armelagos

Cooking is like love. It should be entered into with abandon or not at all.

Harriet Van Horne

Dreams nourish the soul just as food nourishes the body. The pleasure of the search and of adventure feeds our dreams.

Paulo Coelho

Friends are like cupcakes in my pantry of memories.

Author unknown

Boredom is the
feeling that everything
is a waste of time;
serenity, that nothing is.

Thomas Szasz

Without another
thing to do
I ate a cupcake
and thought
of you.

Lois Kaufman

Happy and successful cooking doesn't rely only on know-how; it comes from the heart, makes great demands on the palate, and needs enthusiasm and a great love of food to bring it to life.

Georges Blanc

Great things
are done by a
series of small
things brought
together.

Vincent van Gogh

nom nom nom

Recipe for Happiness

1 measure of a life well lived
1 cup sweetness and light
2 tablespoons levity
1 teaspoon extract of gratitude
1 grain of salt

Mix well, then place in preheated oven. Sit in meditation until more than half-baked. Cool, and top with meringue whipped into a frenzy. Enjoy!

Barbara Paulding

If you want to
stay sane, laugh often
and have a cupcake!
Remember to stop and
savor the frosting.

Author unknown

*A good cook
is like a sorceress
who dispenses
happiness.*

Elsa Schiaparelli

In the sweetness of friendship let there be laughter, and sharing of pleasures.

Kahlil Gibran

Small pleasures—
a walk in the woods, a hot
bath, a hug, a delicious
cupcake—can recharge
body and spirit.

Lois Reynolds

Cooking is an art and patience a virtue. . . . Careful shopping, fresh ingredients and an unhurried approach are nearly all you need. There is one more thing—love. Love for food and love for those you invite to your table.

Keith Floyd

Sweetness is one of the five basic tastes and is almost universally regarded as a pleasurable experience, so enjoy your cupcake.

Evelyn Beilenson

When we sip tea,
we are on our way
to serenity.

Alexandra Stoddard

A balanced diet
is a cupcake in
each hand.

Lois Kaufman

Good things come to
those who wait.
GREAT things come to
those who bake!

Author unknown

God grant me the
serenity to accept the
things I cannot change;
courage to change the
things I can; and the
wisdom to eat a cupcake.

*(with apologies to
Reinhold Niebuhr)*

There is no love
sincerer than the
love of food.

George Bernard Shaw

The aim of life is to live, and to live means to be aware, joyously, drunkenly, serenely, divinely aware.

Henry Miller

Life! Can't live with it, can't live without it.

Cynthia Nelms

Nobody's last
words were
"I ate too many
cupcakes."

Evelyn Beilenson

The more
you praise and
celebrate your
life, the more
there is in life
to celebrate.

Oprah Winfrey

Savor all life's flavors, best enjoyed while still warm. They're the icing on the cupcake.

Barbara Paulding

Food is not about impressing people. It's about making them feel comfortable.

Ina Garten

If more of us valued
food and cheer and song
above hoarded gold, it
would be a merrier world.

J. R. R. Tolkien

Food can look beautiful, taste exquisite, smell wonderful, make people feel good, bring them together, inspire romantic feelings . . . At its most basic, it is fuel for a hungry machine.

Rosamond Richardson

Cupcakes are cheaper than therapy, and you don't need an appointment.

Author unknown

What I love about cooking is that after a hard day, there is something comforting about the fact that if you melt butter and add flour and then hot stock, it will get thick! It's a sure thing! It's a sure thing in a world where nothing is sure. . . .

Nora Ephron

The gentle art of gastronomy is a friendly one. It hurdles the language barrier, makes friends among civilized people, and warms the heart.

Samuel Chamberlain

Learn to be quiet
enough to hear the
sound of the genuine
within yourself so
that you can hear
it in others.

Marian Wright Edelman

*Calmness
of mind is one
of the beautiful
jewels of
wisdom.*

James Allen

Be humble as the blade of grass that is being trodden underneath the feet. The little ant tastes joyously the sweetness of honey and sugar.

John Ruskin

One cupcake
is equal to a
thousand words.

Author unknown

So long as the sugar is on the tongue, you feel the sweetness in taste. Similarly, so long as the heart has love, peace, and devotion, you feel the bliss.

Sri Sathya Sai Baba

Make cupcakes, not war!

Author unknown

The most important
things to do in the world
are to get something
to eat, something to
drink and somebody
to love you.

Brenda Ueland

Practice random acts of kindness. Make the world a better place, one cupcake at a time.

Author unknown

Why are we here? We exist not to pursue happiness, which is fleeting, or outer accomplishment, which can always be bettered. We are here to nourish the self.

Deepak Chopra

Enjoy the little things, for one day you may look back and realize they were the big things.

Robert Brault

When from a long
distant past nothing
subsists after the things
are broken and scattered,
the smell and taste of
things remain.

Marcel Proust

Cooking is
at once child's
play and adult joy.
And cooking done
with care is an
act of love.

Craig Claiborne

Sharing food with another human being is an intimate act that should not be indulged in lightly.

M. F. K. Fisher

If you can spend
a perfectly useless
afternoon in a perfectly
useless manner, you have
learned how to live.

Lin Yutang

*Life is short—
have your
cupcake and
eat it, too.*

Lois Kaufman